Plum Delight

Poetry of the Earth

and
Photography
by
Jean Ann Shirey

*For since the creation of the
world... Romans 1:20*

Jean Ann Shirey

Plum Delight
Poetry of the Earth

by Jean Ann Shirey

Photography by Jean Ann Shirey

Copyright 2019 Jean Ann Shirey

Lamb's Ear Publishing

Library of Congress Control Number: 2019901127

ISBN: 9780997985580

Scripture taken from the NEW AMERICAN STANDARD BIBLE®, ©Copyright 1960, 1962, 1963, 1968, 1971, 1972, 1973, 1975, 1977, 1995 by The Lockman Foundation. Used by permission. www.Lockman.org

Dedication

Plum Delight is dedicated to God through His Son, Jesus, who gave me a home with children, family, church, friends, trees, plants, animals, birds, a town with parks, some travel, and all the mysterious love contained in these pages.

Acknowledgements

I would like to thank my editor, Caitlin Smith Waits, for her generous assistance. Her part in this work is vital. I am grateful for the abilities of my graphic designers, Kim Giles (By Design) and Elysia Brady.

Jean Ann Shirey

*A young cardinal is in the wild plum tree flowers below the center of the title on the cover of *Plum Delight*. The cover photo was taken by Jean Ann Shirey.

The photographs on page 81 were taken by Wallace E. Martin, beloved brother of Jean Ann Shirey.

Page 87 features Showboy, a Holland Lop Grand Champion Rabbit. Showboy was cherished by his owner, Gail Moore.

To the Reader

Enjoy a taste of my life

and all of yours!

Jean Ann Shirey

Table of Contents

Plum Delight

20 *For since the creation of the world His invisible attributes, His eternal power and divine nature, have been clearly seen, being understood through what has been made, so that they are without excuse.*

Romans 1:20

New American Standard Bible, Updated Edition

Plum Delight

The plum tree snowed
light, fragrant, white blooms
at the foot of my garden
and hung softly on
full covered branches.
I joined winged creatures flocking,
intoxicated with my nose
in sweet, plum rose delight,
and I breathed.
I gazed at you in the morning,
and watched you glowing
through the night,
dressed in lace and glory.
You rained on my porch,
as I walked a petal-strewn path
through the season of your time.

The Cardinals

love singers

pass sweet

time partners

feeding one

another sustained

winged dance

mood cherish

alter glistening

light noting

love singers

carry

Moon Flower Shadows

Candlesticks in the air

rising to the moon,

white glistening trumpets

heralding the King.

Sound the night,

sound the day,

the moon flower sings

in foreshadows quiet

until the trumpets

ring the earth.

Sunflower

Proud lady, I can almost hear you sigh,

a giant queen rising high in the sky.

At dawn you looked the sun full in face

and bowed your head in unmatched grace.

But then, I saw the bold look in your eye;

You turned to watch him ride out of the sky.

P.B. Glorious

Surprised with a flash

of bright in a tree

caught to curious glance,

but no,

not a parakeet flown.

Body of songbird,

what is your name?

Colors poured,

sings like no other ...

Painted Bunting, glorious,

come again.

Ode to Spring,

paint the world.

Toddler Blew

first directed breath

puffs above

pudgy fingers firmly held stem

spherical wonder

surprising reward

delightful sounds

to the chase

Dandelion seeds

flew quickly.

A Geranium Bloomed for Easter

Such a sweet

surprise

that lovely pink bloom

heading up

and looking down,

both shy and confident,

greeting me first

on a resurrection day,

reminding me of new life

and great joy,

in a crème-yellow pot

on my kitchen window sill.

The Wisteria Met the Trumpet Vine

The Wisteria met the Trumpet Vine,
and knurled entangles twist
bright greeting of flowers before me,
orange as sunrise on the mist.
Curved but simply stated,
you bring your own display,
while the Wisteria matched your strength.
Climbers both you crawl,
leaping heights into the sky.
Wisteria, you hang your lovely head
with purple tears of joy,
and no one ever made your likeness
sufficient to your day.
So here is the question after you met.
Do I take you both back home,
or trust it is right to let you mingle?
Will you be better as one?

11

Wild Plums on a Tree

Fruit laden balls

of Christmas in August,

decorate spiked branches

beginning fall festivities

with green-leafed, red delights.

Aged brothers

stand in her joyous beauty,

gaining their fill

of tart, succulent fruit,

spewing pits

and good-natured laughs,

spreading the bountiful earth

with wild plum trees

as plum butter

on a piece of winter toast.

Aunt Hallie's Fern

Too frail to carry any longer,
from 90-year-old hands,
the gifted fern came to me,
love in fronds green.

Huge and lovely,
petted and cajoled,
she brought joy.

But alas,
sometimes it was not so,
over fertilizing once
and an unexpected frost
made her bitten brown.

Never defeated,
returned
more bold, green,
slow and steady progress
until she surpassed

the former glory.
She thrives especially
in Spring and Fall
but lasts through any time.

The indomitable will
of God's Spirit of love
expressed through
Aunt Hallie's fern.
May we always be so moved.

Hummingbird

You came back today

and were welcomed

with your favorite meal.

You fight so much,

amazing pilots- bombing,

diving, and defending.

Delicate and quick,

so close

I can feel the draft

of your wings.

Then far away to see

the full extent

of your maneuvering,

soaring and zooming

to great heights

with movements

of flight unmatched

and an added dimension

to my world.

You summer with me

every year.

Lamb's Ear

Eyes wide,

mouth slightly open,

slight shiver

from fingers to heart.

Ahhh.

A child just touched

a Lamb's Ear, plant

of lamb, soft fuzz.

Sunset

Streaks of sky

surrounded me

in blue and dappled orange,

color glows

set over all the world

including me.

I love the heightened

outline of flow

infused with sights

and warm hues

with the golden air,

the taste of sunset.

Pomegranate Tree

Sudden growth
from forgotten seeds,
ancient forms
that graced The Temple,
brought to me
one summer day
to the amazement
of songs, dances,
and prayers
of gratitude,
anchored precariously
on my hill's home.
Reminding me
of my true home,
while decorating the world
with healing.

Christmas Plum

Spiked and barren,

cold and blustery,

winter's chill was in the air.

Warmth could not penetrate

the wounds of thorns impaled,

while you sound out

the beating of the nails

with your branches

against the house,

reminding us of foretold death

while we celebrate

the birth of God's Son,

the coming of God with us.

You with penetrating thorns,

attend our celebration

becoming our Christmas tree,

while He saw into our souls
and died upon a tree
for love of all people.

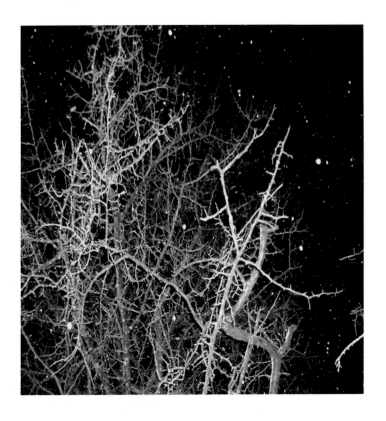

Miracle Day

Rarely snow graces our land,
so when large flakes landed outside softly,
people streamed to revel
in the frosted world.
The temperature was warm,
and the next day snow melted quickly.
I rounded a hill to the surprise
of unexpected wonder,
facing land covered with a wall
of upward cedar trees,
snow clinging to branches
with green scallops outlining
the bright, lovely white,
hill after hill with inches of deep white.
Bluebonnet's recent blooms
of royal blue-purple with white dots
rising above the snow carpets
peered delicately at me.

By the time I arrived at

the church on Easter morning,

I was in an unbelievable state.

I gazed out the window

of the church to the scene

with country trees and fields

covered with white

while sounds of praise lifted

high our voices.

My son said, "Oh, you entered

church with the proper sense of awe?"

"Yes Jonathan."

May we always enter

with the proper sense

of Jesus' resurrection miracle,

with our mouths open

in awe of our Creator,

expressing our grateful love.

May we remember

to listen and ponder.

Surprise Resurrection

Winter land scene before me

drenched in life changing awe,

soaking wonder of altered forms,

breathing outlines of covered

familiar shapes in new snow,

driving through a picture

of unexpected beauty.

I went to worship and was changed

by love's clear form

serendipitously anchored

in me from God.

Poppies

Poppies all

over my yard,

red pops

of drama,

outlined yellow

and black.

It bothers me

much to know

that what was good

was brought low,

but in this land,

it is not so.

Snap Dragon

Moving in the land

side to side,

early battle

history with man,

colorful body,

defined face,

open mouth

for waiting fingers.

They leave and return.

Snap, snap, snap Dragon.

Ahhh! Ohhh!

Want to see the Dragon?

Remember?

Snap Dragon!

Pansies

Tiny little faces,

short ones,

fluttering in the breeze;

colorful personalities

staying from fall to spring.

You all like the cool weather,

never wearing your coats

but wilting in Southern heat.

Vapors, delicate ones,

vapors.

Hydrangea

Such wonderful form

and grace,

shapely and elegant,

a model

of world fame.

You age well,

and your usefulness

continues.

You adapt,

changing into perfect colors.

However, you are

very thirsty.

The Barn Swallows

The swallows nest each year
just outside my window.
It is joy to watch them near
to gather and to grow.
One year a young one fell,
and cats were kept at bay.
As night began to fall,
it was placed in the nest.
I never knew the outcome
but hoped for the best.
All our young ones are gone,
and my husband died this year.
Still swallows entertain,
though rafters begin to fall.
Barn dwellers stayed with me,
and Jesus is always near,
bringing gifts like swallows,
such little birds to bring joy.

What Time Is It?

Sweet perfume

around the house

and down the whole street.

It must be 4 o'clock.

Fluted horns,

open sweet treats,

pastel rainbow ice.

It must be 4 o'clock.

Whirring birds

and insect wings

buzzing in to see.

Is it 4 o'clock?

Children ask,

"How do flowers

know when to open?

"Your name is 4 o'clock?"

God made them

to open wide

almost every day

to view at 4 o'clock.

Plum Snow

Turning the corner,
and there she blew
scented, delicate flakes,
white, falling,
swirling,
entreating,
around the garden,
in my hair,
my clothes,
infusing me,
effervescently wondering
at the spring snow.
Arms stretched out,
around and around,
making snow angels
in a twirl.
Who knew?
The last spring snow
is wild plum flowers!

The Poet of Raby Park

Raby Park

I went down to Raby Park

in the shadows of the sky.

I saw my love in the hills

and kissed my heart good bye.

I thrilled to the creak

of the tall cedar tree

and saw branches flow

to the ground.

I went up white iris stairs

and waved in the tender breeze.

Flying Diamonds

Sun's outline

of light on branches

gives hope of all things new.

Seeing clearly

with brilliance infused

brings joy of forms

unexpectedly precious,

earth's diamonds

to the sky.

42

Thanks

It is a glorious,

wonderful, perfect

day with

butterflies flittering,

tree limbs breezing,

puppies bounding,

and my heart so glad

to see

the perfectly beautiful,

lovely day

with me.

Iris Place

Red plum blooms,

translucent in

evening rays,

in Trinity form

sang first

in Raby Park

today.

Hi Dot

Little weed flowers,

white stars with yellow centers,

you polka dot the hills.

White polka dotted hills

and lovely Spring thoughts.

Oyster Row

Shell embedded

cobblestones from

oysters far away.

You landed

at my feet

in cobblestoned

oyster rows.

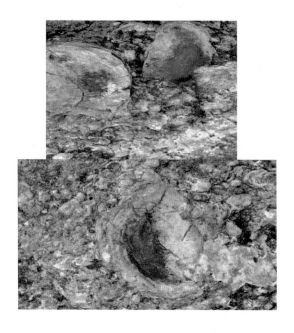

Covered Rock

Green you lay, still in stream

looking up at me

from cold and clear your perch,

while I roll by your lair

my head in the sky,

and you at my wandering feet

while earth wears us

both smooth.

Butterfly Spring

Yellow flitters

up and down

thrust out and

quickly gone,

while you flutter

white with gentle ease

beside my feet

walking me home.

The Setting

I saw your shadow

in the stream

after the sun had set,

golden glaze with peach tones

and a hint of violet.

You held the curve

of the stream while

branches meandered across,

just a toast of loveliness

for such a quiet clear.

Walk of Winter

I love the sweet crackle of leaves,

the swishing gurgle of the spring,

thrill to see shadows on my hands

and steps with small fossils inlaid.

I notice the brick ladybugs and

the green of the moss covered bend,

smiling at the curve patterned tree roots

flowing near the surface of the bank.

I'm refreshed by the walk of winter,

warmed by sun over the cool breeze.

Walk of Winter – too

Sweet crackle of leaves,

swishing gurgle of spring,

shadows on hands,

steps with fossils inlaid,

brick ladybugs, and

green moss covered bend.

Curve patterned tree roots

flowing surface bank.

Walk of winter warmed by sun

over the cool breeze.

Lovely

Long necks in sway,

pale beauties,

delicate and fair,

always constant,

you stand and grace

everyone you meet.

Stately match,

you rise in unison.

Iris, you are called

one and all.

So, why do Iris

have beards?

The Acorn

Little acorn,

with your cap on tight,

you meet the winter chill,

but I noticed

that you tipped your hat

to greet Miss Daffodil.

Ancient Beauty

Ornamental jingles

twinkle in the air,

across the Himalayas,

China sounds, or India.

Good tidings abound

from the Ambassador,

the Texas Umbrella,

in the center of the park.

By the abandoned bath house

grows the high, straight tree

with clusters of florescent

orange-cream-ochre glowing balls

of long stemmed multiples,

hanging for winter cheer.

Through Spring, it waits for sighs

of loveliness beheld

to ponder great beauty,

the China Berry Tree.

China Berry Tree???

You made the #1 hit list

for Exotic Pest Plant,

called invasive and disruptive.

Alas, it is grim to see.

You are so beautiful,

but poison runs in your veins.

In a more perfect world,

it would not be.

Still, it gives me comfort

that you have not run amuck

in Raby Park.

Perhaps the land is hard enough

to keep a despot at bay,

to let him mingle,

but not overthrow.

Grape Hyacinth

Splashes of royal pixie color

billowing forth

a mini world

to catch glimpses

of the peering

mini grapes waving

the grand opening

of spring.

Live Oak Tree

Bold moves,

twists and turns

with massive

upward strength.

Wrinkled skin,

lines and depth,

wise of world,

your name exemplifies.

You rose and

gestured to me.

You waited,

and I stayed.

Rose of Sharon

Lion heart,

versatile,

maneuverable,

hearty,

uplifting,

strong,

amusing,

quick,

leader,

open,

creative,

bright,

flowing,

dear,

beautiful,

wonderful,

glory,

expansive,

fruitful,

and conquering;

you remind me

of someone else

I know.

Movement Tree

Tree patterns on grass

of green shadows

moving in delicate

shaded form.

Canvas of subtle strokes

with etched clarity,

flowing mass carpet

swaying gently,

highlighting sun,

sky, tree, and earth

in a joyous harmony

of musical form.

Tree Stump

Tree stump

with vines

ensuing;

outspreading

tendrils wildly coiffed.

Diseased, cut,

and striding again,

last moment

spreading cheer.

Leaf Dance

I love air on leaves

move

fluff dance

on trees,

jangle light

easy day

sway.

A Fan Letter

You rose to greet each challenge,

holding,

working talents

to their greatest extent.

You are magnificent

in every way.

Although your genus

is obvious;

bloodline

worked in your favor.

You used your gifts

to take the lead

at the head of Raby Park.

Hackberry salute.

Weeping Willow

I saw your tears

as I walked by,

falling softly

from your sky.

Somehow your gentle sway

comforted me

with tender touch

from such great height,

and yet, you reach

to earth walkers

with wistful strokes.

The Mushroom

What a guy,

the fungi among us,

so delectable and sweet,

but watch

what you choose

lest you die

from the not too much ... .

At Home

Two peer into a large pipe

in discovery of love.

A father throws a Frisbee

with his daughter and a poodle

while the disk lands in the stream.

A birthday party picnics;

a husband pushes children

on the tire swing around

while his wife watches laughing.

A man walks two large dogs.

Children laugh on the slides.

Teens work on the skateboard,

and I wander the park.

Country
Estate

Cypress by the Lake

Cypress trees, feet in water,
knees in the air,
soared ascending
branches to the sky.
Scented cones of cypress smell,
spring balls of light-dark patterns
with feathered mists of green
surrounds, leaf halos branching out.
You stand a mountain tree,
planted delicate as firm.
Huge and mighty, gracious beauty,
no bend, but moves you make,
with weathered bark, patterned ridges
that sing and flow away
straight from the trunk
with circled mosaics.
You are erect, a beauty laid,
a pleasure to watch and know.

Little Swimming Frog

The pink with yellow-centered
water lilies held my attention
as a spiked contrast
to their broad, slit leaves,
flat on the water's edge.

Then, up you jumped
on the rocks below,
a little postage stamp
leaping buildings,
sunning, resting.
You jumped and swam
with feet stretched out
so long for you.
Fast as I could think,
you went,
little, swimming frog.

You won the race,

I declare you, Ace,

fast on land or water,

and a dragonfly blue

lay down nearby

on a pink and yellow lily day.

The Fishing Buddies

I met my Daddy

on the fishing boat

in the early rays of dawn,

and out we paddled,

well, just him mostly,

to where the fish were like dew.

Ringing bells of whirring lines,

reeling intertwined

with hook and net,

and "Look how great!"

Truly, I met my Daddy

on the lake, and we always

love each other!

Cardinal Surprise

While walking gently

through the low garden

along the rock strewn way,

lost in thought,

absorbing flowers,

a swift flutter–

just to let me see

a Cardinal moment

with you close to me.

I could almost touch

your nest before me

as you lay hidden

in the curve of the arbor.

What a Cardinal surprise!

A Butterfly Landed on my Paper

A butterfly landed on my paper.

Not wanting to disturb,

I took a walk with You,

which is what You wanted anyway.

We looked, watched, waited

along the path,

and returned again to view.

The butterfly moved all over the paper

with restful wings of grays, browns,

and cream dots among gentle curves

of duplicate, complex patterns

until it flew away; and

I wrote about You again.

Hibiscus Gazing

Hibiscus gazing,
wet and wonderful,
stamen pushing up,
singing tunes
of splendor laid,
colors bold of symphony.

You could carry the land
on your own with great ease
and full the world would be,
with colors wild and brilliant
with hues soft and free.

Hibiscus gazing near to me;
I'm gazing back to thee.

Statue of Children with Rabbit

Clearly I see you

still in statue

stroking rabbit,

filled with awe.

You capture

long past moments

of when my children

played with glee.

The Great Emerald

Little duck,

I saw you fly;

green necked wonder,

here's to you

with your emerald jewel.

Your neck was forward.

Your wings were back,

a vortex bursting upward,

and then you settled

on the lake,

comfortable as great.

Duck Lines

Amphibian airship:

duck water, duck land,

and duck air.

We beheld you

honk.

You honked.

We heard,

"Get out of the way!"

So, that is why

you honk?

So that is why you honk!

The Geese – Balrap

Swimming, swimming,
glide and graceful,
beautiful necks
carved and lovely,
moving together
side by side,
synchronized perfection
with only a tufted crown
to tell you apart.
Ballet in water
breaking gold with white light
upon the lake before me.

Then, you came upon the land.

(Walking away in unison.)

Right, left, right, left,

right, left, right, left.

Ouonk, ouonk, cronk, cronk.

(Look to the right!)

Ouonk, ouonk, cronk, cronk.

(Look to the left!)

Ouonk, ouonk, cronk, cronk.

(Look at each other!)

Ouonk, ouonk, cronk, cronk.

(Forward once again!)

Ouonk, ouonk, cronk, cronk.

Who knew?

Geese ballet in water,

and geese rappers on land!

The Children's Playhouse

What a delectable idea,

to place the children's playhouse

in the garden for teas,

toys, frogs, and lily pads,

to pass the time away

while the children play

like "grown-ups,"

and the adults

relax like children.

The Snake

We didn't want to see you,

but there you were today,

making your journey

from homestead to lake

over the road before us.

Your span filled the path,

and our hearts beat faster to see,

but not as if we had to meet.

This was not a greeting,

just a happenstance fleeting

for both of us!

Excursions

Man of War

We walked the beach again,
as when the boy held my hand
and played, moving back and forth
on this very shore.
We watched mysteries then and now.
The man beside me rose and,
keen-eyed, marvels beheld.
I lifted sand with my toes,
barefooted, playful, through soft foam.
Cool wind, warm sun
was shining on white shells
and my uplifted hands.
Memories of emotions
held a lightness of Spirit
and peaceful waves;
a child wonder-grazed.
A clear, iridescent bladder
lay before us, waiting.
At home in sea to sting its prey,

scarring men for life,
at war with man to death.
Etched in sand,
carved, careful delicacies,
gentle marks of
tentacles laid hidden
just beneath the surface.
You are dying,
and we are living today
to shells awaiting our touch.

Only a mystery, our time,
your stings provoked will take us down
until we walk with our best Friend,
carver of our life,
and meet each other
once again and free,
free of stings of surface laid,
free to meet and be.

Sky and Sea

Amazing sky and sea

as far as the eye can see

to the curve of the earth

or light years away.

The big dipper above

or the waves,

a lifelong introduction

from youngest days,

mass containers of treasure

to search and consider.

There is nothing quite like

the sky and the sea,

and their effect on me.

Girl in Tree

She read

in a red berry tree

far away,

hidden in leaves

and dreams.

No one noticed

until she called

from the perfect place,

the girl

in the red berry tree.

Grackles

Grackles,

cackles,

lackles,

tackles,

wackles,

rackles

in mass

overwhelming the trees,

and the earth.

Yuckles.

Checkerboard Chicken

You bring

delight of movement

across the ground,

followed by my smiling gaze

at your patterned,

graphic design.

You are laughter

with a touch of whimsy.

Checkerboard Chicken II

I love to see

the checkerboard chicken,

game bird of the year!

Do you play chess?

Maple Seeds

I watch them

come down,

twirling,

swirling,

flying through the sky.

The God who laughs

sends toys from on high.

Hawks

I have watched you

through the years,

filling my heart with awe

at your strength,

grace, and determined,

sharp watch.

You soar

to outstanding heights,

and I fly,

your loft aware.

The Fox and the Roadrunner

Confirmation,

the unlikely pair

informed us

of God's continuing,

amazing favor

on Granny,

when they

made frequent appearances

at her suburban patio.

We were always in wonder

at the grace

of God on Granny.

For You

Let me sing
like the bird
You made.

Let me sing
throughout
eternity.

Let me sing
with the voice
You gave.

Let me sing
for You.

In Gratitude

I lived to see a bit of earth

in land, sky, and sea.

Though there is so much,

I quite enjoyed the view.

Should I live a thousand years

or leave this plane today,

I know it will be the same

as I travel home with You.

1 In the beginning was the Word, and the Word was with God, and the Word was God.

2 He was in the beginning with God.

3 All things came into being through Him, and apart from Him nothing came into being that has come into being.

John 1:1-3 NASB

Updated Edition

Isn't it wonderful to notice the Earth?

What an opportunity to meet our Creator!

God sent his Son, Jesus,

to Earth to show the love

God has for all of us.

16 "For God so loved the world,

that He gave His only begotten Son,

that whoever believes in Him shall not

perish, but have eternal life."

John 3:16

NASB, Updated Edition

4 In Him was life, and the life was the Light of men.

John 1:4

NASB, Updated Edition

If we choose to love our Creator,

we come to Him through Jesus, the Word,

the element of creation.

God is waiting for us to love Him back

by receiving Jesus.

*****

12 But as many as received Him, to them

He gave the right to become children of God,

even to those who believe in His name.

John 1:12

NASB, Updated Edition

Will you give your life to God
through His Son, Jesus?

No one can be good enough to go to
God. God let His perfect Son, Jesus, die in
our place for our wrong actions. Each
person has an opportunity to live
abundantly now and forever in heaven.
Jesus came alive again.

Jesus is alive today and forever!

Yielding to God through Jesus, results in
miraculous changes while giving every
follower a complete and joyful life. Talking
to God through prayer and reading the Bible
gives the daily direction we all need. God
offers His specific blueprint for love
throughout the Bible. We are sad about any
behavior that did not match God's standards
in the Bible. We ask God's forgiveness about
our own personal failures to follow His ways.
We ask for Jesus' help to obey Him with
gratitude because of God's great love for us.
God hears our prayers and will be with us.

29 The next day he saw Jesus coming

to him and said, "Behold, the Lamb of God

who takes away the sin of the world!"

John 1:29

NASB, Updated Edition

We come to know Jesus as our Savior and friend. We pray to God in the name of Jesus, communicating everything to Him. Jesus cares for us and has direction for every question that arises in life. A growing relationship develops between God and each person who loves Jesus by the power of the Holy Spirit. Giving ourselves to Jesus is the greatest adventure of life!

14 And the Word became flesh, and dwelt among us, and we saw His glory, glory as of the only begotten from the Father, full of grace and truth.

John 1:14

NASB, Updated Edition

I congratulate each person who chooses life by receiving Jesus. Follow God's leading to a church where God the Father, the Son, and the Holy Spirit are loved as well as believed. May God bless and keep you forever in your decision to love Jesus, the Lord of all!

Jean A. Shirey

Jean Ann Shirey has four married children and eighteen grandchildren. She is so thankful for this bountiful earth and the fruit that God has given. "I noticed nature my whole life. Its reflections altered me."

Jean Ann graduated from Baylor University and worked in the Texas Department of Criminal Justice for 22 years. She was employed by The University of Texas Medical Branch–Insititutional Division for many of those years.

Made in the USA
Columbia, SC
06 March 2022

57068058R00071